MW01514781

A ~~TAIL~~ TALE OF

TWO DOGS

Birgit Stubblefield

Debra Wagner

- BhP -

Brandenburg, Kentucky

BEARHEAD PUBLISHING

- BhP -

Brandenburg, Kentucky
www.bearheadpublishing.com

A ~~Tail~~ Tale of Two Dogs
by Birgit Stubblefield and Debra Wagner

Copyright © 2013 Birgit Stubblefield and Debra Wagner
ALL RIGHTS RESERVED

Cover Design & Layout by Bearhead Publishing
First Printing - September 2013
ISBN: 978-1-937508-21-0
1 2 3 4 5

NO PART OF THIS BOOK MAY BE REPRODUCED
IN ANY FORM, BY PHOTOCOPYING OR BY ANY
ELECTRONIC OR MECHANICAL MEANS,
INCLUDING INFORMATION STORAGE OR
RETRIEVAL SYSTEMS, WITHOUT PERMISSION
IN WRITING FROM THE COPYRIGHT OWNER/AUTHOR

Proudly Printed in the United States of America.

A ~~TAIL~~ TALE OF

TWO DOGS

Dedication

To Sabo and Lily-
for opening the doggy door to love

Lily
Debra Wagner

I accidentally bought a dog. I never intended for it to happen, but fate had other ideas. I went to the pet store to get food for my cats and that is where this weird occurrence happened. I had been a cat lover for over 20 years and was damn proud of it. As I wandered by the

1

dog cage area, I saw a small furry thing running back and forth in front of the caged dogs and I thought "Oh what a cool toy- my cats will love chasing after that!".

I asked the pet store employee where they kept those toys so I could buy one- she had the nerve to laugh at me and told me that was a dog. A DOG??? It couldn't be any bigger than a few ounces- how was that possible? And then the Twilight Zone episode began- I heard myself asking to see that tiny dog. Inside my head I was screaming "What are you doing?? You have four cats!! You are not a dog person!!" But she got out this tiny little furball and put it in my hand and told me it was a Pekingese puppy- it didn't even fill my whole hand. As I examined this strange anomaly something bizarre happened. I lifted her up to my face and she licked my nose (the dog not the pet store employee!). Then things got even stranger. Her saliva had obviously been dosed with some sort of date rape drug, because I found myself pulling out my checkbook and writing a check with lots of zeroes on it. The next thing I knew I was pulling up at home with a cardboard box that contained a tiny furry dog. What the hell had just happened???

And so began my foray into the wide world of dog ownership. I had not intended to buy a dog. I NEVER wanted a dog. I had done no research into the breed to find out its quirks, its needs, or even if this little puppy liked cats or not! And even more horribly, I had not discussed it with the four cats that allowed me to live with them. This was going to be a real hard sale to them. Time for the big guns of persuasion- tuna.

Once all the introductions were made I did the research and found out that my new Peking-ese dog was going to grow up to be a mop. One of those tiny little mops that walk bowlegged in the dog shows. This just kept getting worse and worse. I already had a mop- and that one did not need feeding or petting!

So Lily just joined the pack of cats and decided to be one of the crowd. She sunbathed, she cried during baths, and had no compunction about eating the kitty turds. (EW!) She chased the cats and they chased her right back- she had no idea she was any different.

As our lives grew together the cats found other homes and she became my only pet. We began to grow closer and I could see her person-ality evolve. She was very sweet and very fun- she would always greet me at the door dancing for me, high-stepping like she was in a parade. I worked at a small office in a small town, so I started tak-ing her to work with me. Twice a day when I took my breaks we walked around the downtown area. She was so cute and so friendly soon everyone knew her name. They had no idea who I was but Lily was the new mascot for our town and my company. And being a Pekingese with a squishy face, she could snore like a freight train. I am talking major decibels here. She used to sleep under my desk in her little doggy bed. I will never forget the look on the face of the UPS delivery man delivering a package to my office when he suddenly heard my desk start to snore!

Again as life changed I was injured in a horrific motorcycle accident and had my leg broken in eight places. I was evacuated to a trauma hospital where scores of orthopedic doctors looked at my torn leg and shook their heads. They finally decided to admit me to the hospital for pain management since they still could not decide what to do with the leg. It honestly looked like ground chuck- something you would find in the meat department at the local grocery store. In the end I stayed there a week and then they slapped a cast on it and sent me home. I was in tremendous pain when I arrived home- I couldn't even put a sheet on top of my leg because it hurt so much. Between the pain and the prospect of being in a wheelchair for several months, I was devastated. I just knew I couldn't do it. But every morning Lily would wake up and nuzzle me to get out of bed because let's face it, the dog had to pee. No matter how long it took for me to get myself in that wheelchair she never had an accident while waiting patiently. She kept me going through the wheelchair, the walker, and finally to the cane that I now use. Lily was my therapy dog, my inspiration, and my cuddlebug. She never gave up on me, and to this day I know she is the reason I am walking again.

In keeping with my gypsy way of life soon Lily and I moved again and found ourselves in Hardin County, Kentucky, in a sweet little town named Elizabethtown. Now E'town, as we locals like to call it, is south of Louisville and is the quintessential southern town. We like to drink sweet tea on our front porches in our rocking chairs and jabber about what the neighbors are doing. We love grits and the Fourth of July. You always run into someone you know when you go shopping in the local Walmart. So this is where Lily and I decided to settle down.

In this process of relocating I had found the perfect house that I decided to purchase. It was close to downtown (don't blink or you would miss it) in the older section and was exactly what suited us. When I finally began the frustrating process of purchasing the house I went through a local mortgage company and was introduced to their loan officer, Birgit Stubblefield. As a former mortgage loan underwriter, I know what's what in the real estate department, and I was curious to see how efficient this loan officer was. And I have to say I was very pleasantly surprised!!

After the closing was done and I had moved into my new residence somehow Birgit and I became friends. And you could not imagine a more different set of friends- I guess opposites do attract!! Birgit is from Germany, she is a tall classy blonde who is always perfectly attired in her neutral colors of black, navy or brown. Me? I am what you would call a free-spirited bohemian- red hair with a purple streak in the middle, sparkly colorful dresses, and even a walking cane covered in rhinestones. (I believe you can never have too much sparkle!) Somehow our souls matched up and we became the very best of friends. When we would go shopping together I would encourage her to find her blouses and dresses in vibrant colors instead of her standard neutral. She always stated that I had all the color she needed! But I was sad to see that there was an empty spot in her life. Birgit talked all the time about her dog Sabo who had passed, and how much she missed him. She even had a collage of pictures of him in her office- I just knew she needed another one to love. Even though we occasionally touched on the topic of finding another dog, she always shied away saying that she just wasn't ready and could not replace Sabo.

One day I noticed that Lily was not her usual buoyant personality. She always had a sensitive stomach, but for two days everything had just run through her system. Day three started out the same way so I called the vet and they said to bring her in. After running tests they discovered she had some kind of intestinal thing going on and she was severely dehydrated. They immediately admitted her to the hospital and set up an IV for her. The doctor told me I should be prepared in case I would have to make a hard decision. I loved that dog with all the fierceness of my heart, and I was not willing to lose her. I stayed with her in the doggy hospital, rocking her while the IV's drained into her leg. If there was any way my blood would have helped I would have opened a vein for her. Three days of agony and then suddenly she opened her eyes and the dazed look was gone and her tail begin to wag. She made it through!! I was so grateful....I could not make it throughout life without my Lily by my side. My son has always said that Lily was his replacement when he left home, and I guess in some ways he was right. Jared was living his own life in Colorado, and Lily was here for me to spoil and nurture. (Okay, yes, I admit it- she did have a sparkly pink dress. Or two)

After Lily recovered from her illness my vet started suggesting that I get a second pet-she said it is much easier if you have two pets in case one of them passes. Of course this had nothing to do with the four kittens they had in a cage in their vestibule. I had to pass right by them every time I took Lily in for Doggy Day Care. I swear they made me wait there longer every time I picked up Lily so I would get attached. The four kittens had been thrown from a car along with their mother, who was killed. The vet team had named them Coach, Prada, Dooney and Bourke. (All you purse connoisseurs out there know what I am talking about!) One of the kittens caught my eye- she was a tortoiseshell named Dooney. Apparently tortoiseshell cats are the redheads of the cat family- or so I was told by one of the vet techs. I told them I could not afford the adoption fee and left it at that. The next time I took Lily in they reduced the adoption fee in half, and the next time it was waived. Finally it was "Well just take her home and see how she and Lily get along". And that is how Dooney came to live with us.

Lily was a real sport about it all- I think because she had been raised with cats. Neither one of us though realized that we had just been invaded by the "Tortie Terror" who really thought she should be the head of the pack. Lily and I just let her think she was in charge and kept the peace that way. And then we were a family of three.

8

The Perfect Dog

Birgit Stubblefield

It has been four long years now that Sabo my beloved St. Bernard/Collie mix has earned his wings and is waiting for us over the rainbow bridge. Sabo was simply perfect. Adopted at the age of 4 months from a non-kill shelter in Germany it was love at first sight. At the first visit to the shelter I could already tell Sabo was of an independent mind which was a challenge I wanted in a dog. He did not jump up and down with joy of having a visitor. On the contrary, after allowing me a quick scratch on his back he took residence on top of his dog house and followed my every move with watchful eyes. Really? Of course I had to have this puppy! My mind was made up that I was going to have this dog. The next day I came back with my husband in tow to have him take a look at Sabo – after all, I wanted him to give his blessing. Little did he know he had no choice; the dog practically belonged to me already! I always wanted a big dog, actually a giant is what I was looking for, and this breed would fit the bill. St. Bernard's are known to be loyal, protective and just wonderful family pets provided one could put up with the amount of hair and drool. Something about a St. Bernard's solid bulk, droopy eyes, lazy walk -and yes the drooling too- made me fall in love with this breed. Sabo's Mom was a huge St. Bernard and Dad was a Collie always looking for a good time. When fully grown Sabo resembled both breeds, with the sweet gentleness of the Collie and the stubbornness of the St. Bernard. We were ready to sign adoption papers. The shelter manager had other ideas; she did not want to adopt a dog out to a military family. Too many times dogs were abandoned when families received military orders to return to the States or dogs were dropped off at the shelter's doorstep. And here I was thinking I would do a good thing adopting from a shelter! After a few heated words we came to a compromise. We would sign a contract allowing shelter representatives to visit our home (this is pretty standard in Germany) and that we would return Sabo to her care if we would have to move and we would not be able to take him along. I ensured her this would not happen and so I happily signed our agreement. A new family member was about to join our household. Unfortunately we had to wait two long weeks to pick up our new puppy due to immunization requirements. On pick up day Benny was re-named Sabo by my husband who was a tanker at that time. Sabo is the name of training tank ammunition and was fitting for this dog. As a bonus he was already housebroken when we picked him up. In no time he became the perfect house dog - playful, great with children, mild mannered and with little bit of a lazy bone. He loved the cold weather and snow in winter. Like a little kid Sabo would roll in the snow or chase little children and take their hats off. Children screaming and running away meant that they wanted to play and were chased even harder. As much as Sabo loved snow he was the most water shy dog I have ever met. He would sidestep puddles – now I have never seen a dog not wanting to go straight for any puddle in sight. Sabo was fearful of water.

Without a doubt, when my husband Bob received his military orders to leave Germany and move back to the States Sabo moved with us. During Sabo's 14 years together with us he accompanied us on several tours and to our final destination in beautiful Hardin County, Kentucky. He lived a healthy and happy life until it was time to depart and say our final goodbye. He was blessed with no medical issues until the end. He was the truest and most loyal companion anyone could wish for; this was one of the saddest and hardest times for my husband and me. His departure left a huge hole in all of our hearts – a feeling I never would have anticipated losing a dog. During Sabo's last days with us, our Veterinarian Dr. Reed was by our side helping us with the most difficult part of our goodbye. Her compassion and love for animals and her care for Sabo had been a great source of support and helped us tremendously. Dr. Reed gently suggested that there are many dogs who deserve to be loved and a new puppy may just be the medicine we need. Our hearts were heavy and a new dog just was not the right choice for us so soon. And time went by. Baxter the cat was still with us and we told ourselves that he deserved our undivided attention and to be the sole beneficiary of our love.

Transitions
Debra Wagner

Right about then I started struggling with owning my house. Between the financial struggles and the maintenance that I couldn't do because of my bum leg, I was quickly becoming overwhelmed. Suddenly out of the blue my son called me from Colorado and invited me to come to Colorado to be closer to him and his fiancée. I was so relieved- and thrilled to be close to my son again. (We had lived in separate states for about 10 years) So I put my house on the market and started packing up to go. The problem was, though, my house didn't sell for 9 months. Once it was all finished, my son Jared flew out from Colorado Springs, packed me, Lily and Dooney in the car- and then- ROAD TRIP! Even though I was excited to be close to Jared again, it was so hard to say good- bye to my Kentucky friends, especially Birgit. I had been truly blessed to have someone like her in my life. I knew she was unique and brilliant and I could never replace her.

We arrived in Colorado and soon settled into our normal routine. There is a whole different tempo to Colorado Springs, which is a huge city of 400,000 people- most of them military. It was difficult for me to find activities to meet other people. And then there was something weird going on with my health. Without going into all the details, I was diagnosed with cancer. Once again my little Lily stood over me as I struggled through the health issues. Although my cancer was not as horrific as others have had to deal with, it still took its toll. Lily would lay in the bed with me while I recovered, when I was too weak to do anything. She would just lay her head on me and look at me with those buggy eyes full of love and understanding. Somehow she knew, once again, that I needed her. And she was there for me. Plain and simple.

As I recovered I began to get out and start learning how to paint. Now you have to know that I couldn't draw a stick figure to save my soul, but the place I went to learn served wine so how bad could it be, right? RIGHT. Okay, so I will never be a Monet or a Renoir, but at least I have learned the difference between the two artists! (Just don't quiz me on them!) And I got the opportunity to paint a portrait of Lily, with a lot of much needed help from the instructor.

I stayed in touch with my friends in Kentucky, especially Birgit. But calling and texting is just not the same. I missed them, and E'town dearly- I realized that I belong in a small southern town not a large mountain city. It didn't help that Birgit had texted me a picture of a sign showing information about an apartment complex that was being built close to her subdivision. (Subtlety is not her forte) But I was determined to make this work- being close to Jared, my only son, was so important to me.

And then grief stepped into our lives with all the stealth of a ninja in the night. One afternoon Lily suffered a seizure, stiffened up, lost control of her bodily functions and passed out. Luckily our vet was only five minutes away and we got her there as fast as we could. After many tests, (and dollars) they were unable to determine the cause and said to just keep an eye on her. In the days that followed, I started to see that my little Pekingese angel was beginning to decline. She was now 11 years old, and just like me, was wearing down. We used to have races to see who could get to the top of the basement stairs first- she even gave me a three stair head start before she raced up past me and waited at the top for Mom to make it. Now she struggled and paused at stairs on the way up. She couldn't jump up on the couch any more- I had to pick her up and put her on the couch. Her eating became sporadic and she started to lose weight. I could see her wasting away and disappearing right before my eyes. When I first got Lily I made her a promise, that when it wasn't fun to be a dog any more, I would take care of it. I have seen people hang on to their pets, using every possible means to save them, and kept them alive too long causing them suffering. I would never do that to Lily. I couldn't.

Lily started spending more and more time under the bed. I have heard that when an animal is sick or knows that it is dying it will separate itself from others. I was praying that this was not true for Lily. And then one morning I got up and Lily came out from under the bed. She immediately threw up bile everywhere, and then her legs buckled underneath her and she couldn't stand. With tears in my eyes I knelt down and picked her up, and knew that it was The Day. I held her in my arms and rocked her like a baby until she gentled down. In my head I replayed all that she had brought into my life- from my first "accidental" purchase of her, to Lily standing by me when I was ill, right down to her annoying loud snoring. Her total unconditional love. I had always said I wouldn't know what I would do if I lost Lily, and I was about to find out.

Once she calmed down I got her leash and put it on her. Lily got all excited-she thought she was going to the vet for her "spa day"- grooming. She began to dance excitedly, and my heart broke. Here she was thinking she was going to have a fun exciting day, and I was going to...well, you know. We got in the car and Lily sat on my leg as I drove the short distance to the vet. I parked the car and could not get out. I broke down completely- tears falling down my face and onto the top of Lily's head. She turned around and began licking the tears from my face. I cried harder. I just could not get out of that car and do this. I finally called my Mom, who is a former nurse and the strongest woman I know. She and Dad had owned several dogs in their lives and been through this experience. Mom told me how important it is to make certain we take care of our fuzzy children and not allow them to suffer. After her words of strength I finally got out of the car.

We walked slowly into the vet. They took

Lily to the back to get a catheter into her leg. The tears were streaming down my face, raining on the papers I was trying to fill out, leaving salty trails. Then they put me in a room and brought Lily in on a pillow. I held her while they depressed the syringe- one little jerk from Lily, and she was gone. I gently kissed her head and took off her collar, clutching it in my hand as I made my way out to the car.

And so Lily Wagner, one week before her 12th birthday, passed from this world. My heart was not broken- it was shattered. This blessed little furball who had been the light of my life- was snuffed out.

Getting Ready
Birgit Stubblefield

I can't deny longing for a new canine companion long before Bob was ready to even entertain the thought of a new household member. And more time went by. Slowly we laughed and enjoyed the antics of neighborhood and TV dogs. Inch by inch we came closer to talking about a new dog – far off in the future. And more time went by. In December 2012 shortly before the Holidays with long evenings ahead of us and really nothing to do to keep us busy but TV I finally turned to my husband and blurted out "Will we ever get a new dog?" After a deep breath and a moment of silence he surprisingly said "We'll look after the Holidays"…..Yayyyyyy!!!! Really? Are you sure??? Oh, how excited and filled with anticipation I was! I would only move forward with this if he was on board too. The search for a new family member started NOW……happy times ahead of us with a furry bundle of joy. I knew my heart was open for a new dog. I knew I wanted to adopt a dog from a dog pound. I knew I wanted a large dog. I knew I wanted a dog different from Sabo. I knew I WANTED A DOG!!! I envisioned a loyal companion, mild mannered, similar in character to Sabo who would accompany me on long walks. It was time to trade in the old treadmill for brisk walks in fresh air exercising my new large breed dog and losing a little weight in the process. And so my search began…

Bob's sister and her husband are dog lovers too and among their six-pack of dogs a beautiful Pyrenees named Kimber had captured my heart. And so I thought to check into a Pyrenees mix. Thank GOD for the Internet. My search began that evening. There are so many sites and so many dogs but luckily Petfinder.com made the search easy. They listed pets from all different shelters and one can search by size, breed, zip code, and male/female. So many dogs, so many choices, but wait…..OH, how cute! A whole litter of Pyrenees/Lab mixes were just listed- a total of eight boys and girls. All of them looking so happy and so innocent but all of them rejected and dropped off at the shelter for adoption. For no particular reason a little boy named Nanook stood out and seemed to look straight into my heart. First search and we have a hit! Could it really be? Emailing back and forth with the shelter it became clear that there was a great demand for these little pups but they would have to remain with the shelter/foster parent for 2 weeks. A visit was not possible until a later time. So what to do? Unseen and on faith, I put a deposit on little Nanook only to see online that he was on hold for someone else. Although ALL of the pups were so cute and all looked almost alike, this is the one I wanted. Why? I don't know. Just a little voice telling me that he was The One. After a frantic email to the shelter on Christmas Eve I received the greatest Christmas present – an immediate email back from the shelter that the wrong person was listed online and that Nanook was really mine. However, his name "Nanook" did not seem quite right and his name would need to change.

.... I have to call my friend Debra in Colorado – she just adopted a furry little kid a few weeks earlier - we would have to compare notes and definitely would have so much to talk about. Wish she was here! Debra and I met during the process of purchasing her new Kentucky home several years earlier and soon became the best of friends. At my first visit to Debra's new home I met Lily, her little Pekingese and I was treated to a little "dance" as well as a cuddle on the sofa. Our friendship was Lily approved and sealed with a snort. Lordy, could this girl snort! A couple of years later Debra, Lily and Dooney - yes, she had a cat too – decided to move to Colorado to be closer to family. It was a sad goodbye but we vowed to stay in touch and always be BFF's. While we stayed in touch and our friendship stayed intact, it just was not the same. One of the most colorful people one can meet with a personality to match, I missed having her around. Vibrant, funny, outspoken and gentle at the same time and ALWAYS making me laugh, I missed her. One day I received the sad news that Lily too had said her final goodbye. Knowing what I went through with my loss I could understand the sadness and lone- liness Debra must feel. I was happily surprised when I received an email with a picture of a little bitty dog with the name of Cricket, Debra's new companion. I was very happy that she had been able to make this choice. I wanted a dog again too! Now that my hus- band was open again for a new dog we would have so much to talk about again and compare notes.

Cricket

Debra Wagner

My home and my heart were empty. When this happened with Lily I was in the midst of packing and moving into a new apartment. The physical labor kept my hands busy but I couldn't seem to focus on anything but my grief. No one to greet me at the door with her high step dancing, no one to snore like a freight train in my ear. For almost 12 years I had shaken her in the night to roll over and stop snoring- now I would give anything to hear that sound again. Even Dooney seemed to realize something was very wrong- she kept going from room to room crying softly as if she was missing Lily too. Night after night I would take Lily's collar and hold it to my heart as I fell asleep, desperately wishing that I could hold her in my arms again, if only in my dreams. When I was a little girl there was a certain doll I wanted for Christmas named Chatty Cathy; I used to believe that if I could dream about her and hold her in my arms as I awoke I would pull her from the dream world into the real world. Even though this never happened there was still that little girl inside of me that believed if I could hold Lily in my arms in my dreams I could bring her back into my world.

With time the move into the new apartment came to pass and I believed it would lessen the pain since Lily had never lived in that apartment, so I wouldn't look for her, right? I continued to hold her collar in my hands when I fell asleep, always making certain that I put her collar under the pillow so that my kleptomaniac cat did not run off with this most precious keepsake. As I awoke one morning and lifted the pillow up, there next to Lily's collar was Dooney's favorite ball of yarn. It seems that I was not the only one missing Lily.

I had talked with both my sisters, Jenni and Susan, about my loss. Jenni had also lost two very precious cats that were her family members as well. She suggested that I take out Lily's portrait that I had painted and hang it on the wall and talk to her. Sounds crazy, right? I told Jenni that I didn't know if I could bear to do that, but I would try. I finally hung up Lily's picture, and our conversations began.

I shared with her how much I missed her, how much she had blessed me. I told her I could never love another as I had loved her. She was my only dog, and had done so much to help me through some very difficult times in my life. I honestly did not know how to move forward. Then one day during one of our "conversations" the thought occurred to me that there are a whole lot more animals out there that needed to have loving homes. I called my sister Susan who had adopted a Chihuahua and chatted with her about the challenges she had experienced with Ripley. As the idea took root in my heart, I realized that I could not honor Lily's memory more than by adopting another dog who needed rescuing. I didn't have a lot of money, but what I DID have was time and a lot of love to give.

So I began "just looking" on the internet. You know how it is- just browsing in the store without any intention of purchasing something. I looked at some Pekingese dogs, and thought about it but realized that another Peke would be too much of a reminder of Lily. Hmmm, so what other kind of dog would I like? Could I really love another dog after Lily? Finally in one of my conversations with Lily I put the ball in her court- I said a little prayer to her asking for her help in finding just the right dog. One that I didn't have to run after with my bad leg, or one who was too hyperactive. And Lily, bless her little heart, didn't take long in sending me the answer.

It popped into my head that a friend of a friend had a Yorkshire Terrier. He was a cute little guy and seemed friendly enough when he finally calmed down. But would that breed be too much for me to handle? So I went back to the internet to do some more investigating.

I started by checking with local breeders to get an idea of what the cost of a Yorkshire Terrier is just for comparison purposes. Imagine my astonishment when I discovered that these tiny little pups were going for $2500 a piece! Next I began looking for local rescue organizations and was pleased to see there were several. I finally located one that specialized in Yorkshire Terriers. I was astonished to find that there were "rules" one had to follow to rescue a puppy mill dog. I would have to sign a contract that I would never crate or carrier my dog, since she would have already spent all her life in a cage. I would need to submit an application for approval, along with pictures of where I lived. As I was scrolling through all these websites and looking at literally hundreds of photos- suddenly- there she was! Just a tiny little mite with a purple bow in her hair and a sparkle in her eye. She was only three years old so she would have many years to share with a new family. I bookmarked her picture and then sent an email to the rescue organization. Now it is time for hurry up and wait.

As I sat around waiting for the company to respond, I did some more searching on the internet for additional information on what to expect when you adopt a rescued puppy mill dog. To my surprise, there wasn't much information other than the standard articles and books on training a new puppy. I was curious to know how this was going to differ from when I got Lily. And then there was the heart issue- can I really love again after having the most incredible little dog in my life? It's like once you have perfect, where do you go from there?

I finally heard back from the rescue organization- yes "Cassie" was still available. Then I hit the first big hurdle- the adoption fee was $325.00!

That was going to be a struggle for me with my limited income but I knew I could find a way. I discovered that this fee was high because it included the cost of her spay, medical exam and first rabies shot. I sent in my application and pictures from my apartment to begin the adoption process. I asked if I could come out to the rescue place and meet this cute little tyke, but was told I would not be able to see her until the adoption went through. But what if our personalities weren't a good fit? I wanted to be certain that this was the right step for all of us, including Dooney. So once again, I waited, and not very patiently.

You would think I was an expectant father pacing the waiting room anxious for news of the big delivery. (Of course, in this day and age Dad had better be in the delivery room getting his fingers broken by a wife in labor who is holding his hand!) I turned on the TV and then turned it off again. I picked up a book and read a chapter only to realize that I couldn't remember anything I had read. I decided to have a talk with the other "kid" in the family- Dooney. Now Dooney had become quite well adjusted to being an only child. She got first priority on a spot on the bed with Mom at night, got all the attention when I came home, and always had an empty lap to jump into whenever she wanted. So I told her that the stork was going to bring us a new baby and she would have to be the big sister. As my parents had always told ME growing up- "You are the oldest so you have to set the example". Dooney simply yawned and walked away in the middle of the big speech. So much for support from that corner.

Finally the call came- Cassie was mine and I could pick her up any time I wanted to!! I was so excited- and then I found out I had to drive all the way to Trinidad near the New Mexico border to pick her up- which is about a 2 ½ hour drive from where I live in Colorado Springs. Now that's a problem- I can't drive that far with my bad right leg. So I called my son and Jared agreed to drive me down on the day after Thanksgiving. (There may have been some emotional blackmail involved in the request.)

I am going to be a new Mom again!!! So much excitement- I jumped in the car and drove to Petsmart to stock up on new dog supplies. A cute pink little bed, a purple collar, potty pads, food....whew this was exhausting but so much fun! I brought it all home and showed it to Dooney, who twitched her tail and turned away. It was a good thing I had brought her a new mousey to play with…. Or I might have had to find another place to live!

The Big Day. I hadn't slept all night in my excitement. (Yes, I was always the kid who woke up my parents at 5:00 am on Christmas morning!) I had been instructed to bring a blanket to wrap the new baby in- no carriers or crates. I was so nervous and excited. I had already started trying to figure out a new name for the new little one. Cassie was pretty but somehow I didn't think that was the right name for my little bundle of joy. I considered "Holly" in light of the season, but thought I should probably meet her and find out what her personality was like before deciding. I just knew Lily was looking down from doggy heaven and smiling- silly Mommy!

We pulled into the parking lot where we were scheduled to meet up with Chris, one of the rescue owners. I jumped out of the car (well, okay, after the long ride it was more of an exuberant hobble) and ran over to the waiting truck. I looked in the front seat and there was this ball of fur rolling and tumbling around- turns out there were three dogs there as another new owner was coming to pick up two other Yorkies. We went through all the paperwork and Chris began to tell me about my new little one. Apparently the conditions where they found the dogs were horrific. Cassie had just been delivered of another set of puppies and her uterus had become infected. Rather than contacting a vet for treatment, the owner was going to drown her the very next day. Thank goodness the rescue group got there in time! I had to ask Chris to please not tell me any more because I was too upset. I just wanted to get this little furball home and change her life into one of love and joy. He did mention that she had a sweet disposition and loved to burrow under the covers at night. His final word of advice? Keep a tight leash on her because caged animals have a tendency to bolt and run if they have the chance.

And the moment came when he laid her in my arms. My first thought was "My goodness, she hardly weighs more than a cricket!" She was so tiny- barely over four pounds, which is underweight for a Yorkie. Her eyes were slightly glazed because she was medicated after her spay, having her uterus removed, and having six teeth pulled. I wrapped her in the blanket and immediately started crooning to her. I wanted her to get used to the sound of my voice.

We returned to the car and began the drive back home. Well, actually, Jared drove and I cuddled. The tiny dog was so very quiet- no squirming or trying to get away at all. About halfway home I realized that I needed a few more things from the pet store so we stopped and went in. Of course I had my new baby in my arms; if you want attention in a pet store just walk inside with an adorable dog in your arms and you are both immediate superstars! We were in the treat aisle trying to determine which of the 4,000 treats would work for her when a lady came up behind us and smiled. Looking at the cute little Yorkie, she asked me her name. I kind of shuffled and said that I knew it sounded strange but I was thinking of naming her Cricket. The lady started laughing and I indignantly thought to myself "Well, it wasn't THAT bad of a name!" She wiped a tear from her eye and still chuckling told me that her grandmother had a Yorkshire Terrier for 15 years whose name was Cricket! I guess that was the Universe's way of confirming to me that her name is indeed Cricket. So we made it back to Colorado Springs with tiny little Cricket in my arms. I dropped Jared off at his house and brought the new little one home. We were once again a family of three. Perfect!

Harper - A New Beginning

Birgit Stubblefield

December 28 – tomorrow is adoption day! Can't wait. And I am prepared! Everything this little pup would need was already in the house waiting for him. From food and bowls to the biggest, softest dog bed and a number of toys. And not to forget – piddle pads and a gate. I had a plan! It would be great! The opinions on piddle pads and gates vary and some recommend kennels. I believed that gating off the kitchen and letting the kitchen be his kennel would work just fine. Another sleepless night - tomorrow we would pick up our new family member.

December 29 – it snowed last night! No!!!! We have a 2 hour ride, will we make it? Yes, Bob assured me we will go, no matter what! We were meeting the foster parents halfway at noon.

Okay it is 12:15 – where are the foster parents? Here comes a car with their description. Here comes my boy – my heart is beating faster. And here he is…..meet Harper!

I could not believe the moment was finally here! Harper looked just like his online picture, and yes, this was definitely the dog I had chosen. He was placed in Bob's arms while paperwork was exchanged and everything finalized. His curious little buttons eyes took everything in but he showed no signs of being afraid of these new people who ahhh'd and oooh'd over him. He seemed curious and happy from the get go. Finally it was my turn to hold my new kid – so light, small and seemingly fragile at 10 weeks young. But good grief he stunk!!! He needed a bath, bad!!! So let's get on the road and take him home. The foster parents assured us that he had adjusted well at the foster home. They let us know that he would even give a little whine when he needed to go potty. Yay…..that was what I wanted to hear! The see through plastic container in the back seat, nicely padded with a soft blanket and a little toy inside seemed way too big for this small dog. Little did I know he would outgrow his travel container within the first two weeks. For now Harper barely could look over the top but that's okay. He was safely tucked away for our 2 hour ride back home. Curious and peeking over the rim of his box we took off to take him away to his new home. Quickly he settled in and went to sleep; reminding me of the car rides we took with our son when he was a baby. Often this was the only way to get our son Chris to go to sleep. The rhythm and sound of the car always made him fall asleep. He is now an adult and will be terribly embarrassed to read this. Payback is sweet! Apparently this method works for dogs too ☺ But good lord the smell of this dog – I am thinking of cow patties – quickly filled the car and settled in all our clothes too.

Two hours later we are home. The moment of truth – how will Baxter the cat react to Harper? Surprise! Baxter is curious and not hiding behind the sofa as I thought he would. Sniffing each other, I guess Baxter realized this thing was here to stay and it was better to be somewhat friendly than to fight it. But that smell was filling the room and something had to be done about it. So off to the bathroom and into the tub – Harper looks like a scared wet rat but doesn't fight it too bad. A warm towel is waiting and his big dog bed is set up ready for him. Too little to climb onto the big bed a little shove helps him settle in and fall asleep. Yes, Harper is the right name for him. And life as we knew it would change.....

Funny how his name came about. Keeping a

running list of possible dog names, none seemed right. Jack – in my mind I see a black Lab, Sherman – a St. Bernard and so on. The inspiration came at the Irish Pub in Louisville and a good tasting beer. Many good things have happened in an Irish Pub – my husband and I were introduced to each other by a mutual friend in the Irish Pub in Frankfurt, Germany. Well, while sitting at the bar toasting Santa Claus with a glass of Harp beer - it was right before Christmas and Santa Claus was sitting next to us and was thirsty too (and a little tipsy) - we discussed our favorite subject of late, what to name the new dog. The mood was light and playful when Bob smiled and announced the dog's name would be Harper. What a GREAT choice – we had a match. Harper it would be.

Day 1 – until now the day was filled with excitement and now the puppy is taking a little rest. I can't believe he is here with us. A cold snowy day outside with a warm fire going inside and it is the perfect picture of tranquility. Bob and I will take turns taking the puppy outside for his potty breaks. And so we keep the heavy jackets, boots and gloves handy. We take him in the furthest part of the back yard to designate an area to Harper's potty activities. As tiny as he is and as cold as it is outside, we carry him outside; carrying him also because the garage door opening startles him. We make at least ten trips to the back yard. The cold and snow does not bother us – at least not on this first day. So cute, a little tinkle and he comes running back to sit at my feet to be picked up again. Perfect, the dog is already coming to us without being called and he is staying close to our side. Life with the new dog will be great. Cuddled up on Bob's lap it is so peaceful in the home and we have three more days we can spend the entire day with Harper cuddling and loving on him before we both have to return to our everyday work life.

It's been such an exciting and emotionally exhausting day and it is time to go to bed now. Harper's bed is in a kitchen corner along with a pillow covered with an old t-shirt. Perhaps the scent of his new human mother will give him security and comfort during the night alone in the kitchen. Off to bed we go expecting a restless night ahead of us. And we are not disappointed…Harper is whining and trying to figure out a way how to trick the gate so it will open up for him. After a while he settles in and goes to sleep. Great! Two hours later again….there is a little whining noise. We are both wide awake and grabbing at our clothes to get Harper outside to take care of his business. Hurry, hurry get the pants and boots, and coat, and gloves and hat! Too late….piddles on the kitchen floor. No big deal- Bob gears up to brace the cold winter night while I am cleaning the kitchen floor. There are many great products on the market to clean and eliminate the scent but diluted vinegar will also do the trick. The bed is still warm and so we go back to sleep….for another couple of hours to get up again and take care of business. Around 6:00 am I can't sleep any longer and smell fresh brewed coffee. Hmmm....I find Bob stretched out with puppy cuddled up on his lap. They've been there on the couch for the past 2 hours!!!! How cute!! And so day 2 begins.

Quickly it becomes clear that puppy needs to go outside A LOT and it becomes a race to put on heavy clothing and boots to take him outside. We watch him like hawks but the one second we look away is the moment Harper's little bladder lets go....ughhhh. We give him lots of praise and treats when he does his potty outside. He sleeps a lot and his preferred spot is Bob's lap. It is already becoming clear that his new Dad is also his cuddle bud. When awake and playing, Harper likes to use his sharp little baby teeth and his preferred chew toy is my hand. Day two is filled with play time, many trips outside, lots of cleaning – I definitely need to stock up on vinegar! As the day is ending we were tired but had fun with our new dog.

Day three is more of the same - I could sit and watch my dog all day long. He loves to sleep cuddled up with Bob but loves to bite my hand whenever he is awake. His razor sharp little baby teeth have a way of tearing into my hand. Ouch! Why don't you let me pet you? This is beginning to be annoying and disappointing. I am reading anything I can find on the internet about raising a puppy and puppy training.

Tomorrow the reality of the everyday life will start back up; tomorrow we will need to go to work. Since Bob leaves the house really early in the morning, I have to figure out how to handle everything and still get ready on time. I am fortunate to have a flexible schedule so I am sure it will be all right.

Next morning I am spending as much time with puppy Harper as I can, including taking him outside. It seems like every 10 minutes he has an accident and will need to be taken outside. Coat and boots on and off is a little cumbersome but has to be done. Oh man, it's cold outside. My treadmill will not get a workout this morning. Little did I know on that morning that our exercise equipment would not be used for weeks to come. When it's time to leave the house I find myself wishing I could spend the day with the new puppy. I will be back during lunch to play and take him outside. In the meantime I hope he will be all right. During lunch I rush home to find several little puddles on the kitchen floor. I show Harper his piddle pad spread out in the kitchen but he takes no interest. How will I make him understand to use the pads instead of the kitchen floor? So out we go to teach Harper where to do his business in the yard. The ground is wet and slushy and it is cold outside. It is evening now and we are not bored watching TV anymore. We are settling in with our dog and it is fun to watch him play and run after the cat. It's not so much fun to clean all the little accidents that seem to happen every 10 minutes. And it is not so much fun to bundle up every 10 minutes to carry Harper to the backyard. It's cold outside!

Holy Jumping Cricket

Debra Wagner

Or not. I read the contract I had signed about not making Cricket stay in any kind of crate or container, but that was about all the information I received on a dog who was in a puppy mill. I put out her food and water and showed her where that was, along with the cute little pink bed. I had purchased a collar for her as well as a harness. The rescue leaders had told me that oftentimes the puppy mill owners would grab a dog by the scruff of the neck to take them out of the cage, so this became very stressful for the dogs to be handled this way. Hence the harness, that was attached to the entire back instead of just the neck. I attached the leash to her harness with the intent of taking her out to go potty. Imagine my surprise when she planted her tiny little tush on the ground and basically refused to go! I understand that it is only 40 degrees out there, but sweetie, we have to go take care of business. She just didn't understand, and piddled right there in the entryway. Well at least I knew her bladder was working.

So I cleaned up the mess and told her that was not the right way to do the potty thing. I bundled her up in my arms again and sat down in my chair to watch TV. I turned the TV on and Cricket about leaped out of my arms!! Strange, unfamiliar sounds- she did not like that at all!! Then the neighbors upstairs started walking around and Cricket almost jumped completely out of my lap again! Oh, dear, this was not going well at all. I looked up and saw Dooney around the corner from where we were sitting, and I could swear she was smirking at me in a most sinister cat-like way. No support there!

I finally decided bed was the answer to this crazy first day together. As we all got into bed, as I had been warned, Cricket burrowed under the covers all the way to the end of the bed. Could she breathe down there? Was she all right? Dooney completely snubbed the little hump under the covers and settled in on the heating pad. (I had bought the heating pad for my bad leg but Dooney decided it was meant for her. I had to go buy a bigger heating pad so my leg could be on it too!) During the long cold Colorado night I did what any new mother would do- I kept checking on the baby. She seemed to be doing fine, and Dooney was ignoring her like she didn't exist. The first night went well- no middle of the night whining or crying.

The next morning- everyone up! I put on my coat and leashed up the dog to go outside and.......nothing. She had no idea what a leash was all about- I ended up dragging her around, and no pottying occurred. After about 10 minutes we went back inside and immediately on hitting the warm air- yup! The bladder was still working. So I again cleaned up and then got out the potty pads. I picked up Cricket and set her down on the pad and......Oh, no- the potty pad makes a crinkly noise! Off the piddle pad and down the hall and under the bed. Well, that sure didn't work.

So let's move on to the next bodily function- eating breakfast. Cricket was underweight so I had bought some of that yummy wet food to help her gain some weight. I mixed the wet food in with the kibble and put it down for her to eat. She was such a little priss about eating- she daintily picked out the wet food and pretty much left the kibble alone. Meantime, Dooney was like a panther on the prowl, crouched behind the plant in the dining room waiting for the truly tasty food to become available. As Cricket delicately stepped out of the kitchen, Dooney rushed in and began scarfing like she had been starving for weeks. (Never mind that she had her own bowl of kibble in the bathroom that was filled and waiting for her!) As Dooney was consuming the wet dog food, Cricket slipped into the bathroom to eat her dessert- cat turds. You have GOT to be kidding me!!

Of course, once the food goes in the other comes out. I was primed and ready- coat in hand, leash ready to go. When oh no, Cricket don't..don't...too late. That is the problem with little dogs- they can assume the position and be done before you have even blinked. Wow, we were doing great- no pottying outside, no pooping outside- I was failing as a doggy Mom. Thank goodness we had an appointment with the vet that day. I could finally get all my answers from an expert!

I had decided to purchase a doggy sling for carrying Cricket around. It is the same premise as a baby sling- holds the dog tight to your front while harnessing the dog in so that she can't jump out. Once the time came for Cricket and I to go to the vet, we began playing our own version of Twister. I would get her all settled in the sling and be ready to harness her in when she would wiggle her way out and then sit there with a big silly doggy smile on her face, like she just won the game. A few more rounds of Twister and then FINALLY we were all bundled up together. Lookout Dr. Vet- here we come!

Poor little Cricket was so afraid of the car-once again a new and unfamiliar experience for her. We made it to the vet and were sitting in the waiting room when all the dogs started barking in the back. Cricket began to shiver- if all the other animals were making noise there must be something truly horrible going on here! Finally we made it back to the room and this is where I finally began to understand about rescue dogs thanks to our vet.

Puppy mill dogs spend all their time inside a cage, 24/7. Cricket had never felt grass, had never played with a toy, had peed and pooped in her own cage, and probably never had enough food to eat which is why she turned to eating turds. These dogs are never on a leash, never exercised, never bathed, never knew the touch of a loving human hand. When people adopt a new puppy, they have to work with the dog to learn new behaviors to be able to fit in with the family. You are working from a clean slate- being able to start from the very beginning teaching your dog how to act. With a rescue dog, you have to UNLEARN the old behaviors before you can teach them new behaviors, a much more difficult task. My vet doctor told me that I would need a lot of patience and consistency to bring my little Cricket to the point of behaving the way I wanted her to.

Well, no one put all THAT in the adoption papers! But I was committed. Now that I had a better understanding of where Cricket was coming from, I could work with those behaviors to bring her around to being the dog she was meant to be- a member of our little family.

Since Cricket had never bonded with a human, that sling became our modus operandi. I took Cricket EVERYWHERE with me for two weeks in that sling. She went with me to painting class (and she was very good!), to put gas in the car, to visit Jared and his wife, to pick up prescriptions at the local drug store. I wanted her to know the smell of me, the feeling of me, to know that she was safe with me. I told her over and over again that she was no longer the Mama but she was instead the baby, and was going to spend the rest of her life being loved and cared for.

Patience, Patience, Patience...
Birgit Stubblefield

And so the first week goes by and we settle into a routine. It is a LOT of work to clean after the puppy and I am thinking that maybe crate training would be the better choice. After all, every professional trainer recommends this method. Bob won't hear of it. I need more vinegar and my kitchen floor smells like salad dressing. Harper too has settled in and is also developing a routine. Around 4:00 am Harper is awake and whines until Bob gets up and cuddles with him. Precisely at the time I join them, Harper wakes up and starts to exercise his teeth. No matter how many chew toys I shove in front of him he wants to bite and chew on my hands. His teeth are sharp as needles and he leaves marks. I don't think the dog likes me very much. Why won't he cuddle with me like he does with Bob? Why does he always bite me and pee in front of me?

I'll ask Dr. Reed at the Helmwood Veterinary Clinic. She'll be surprised to see me with a new dog after all these years. I know she will have the answer for me.

In the meantime I am looking to the internet to

find answers. What I am finding does explain why he likes to chew my hand but does not really offer a solution or a fix. Giving puppies a variety of chew toys is what is mostly recommended. Honestly, this does not work - at least not for me. The dog likes to bite me and I don't know what to do about it. While on the Internet, I find a couple of promising dog training websites. It may still be early for Harper but I know I want the best trained dog I can get and so I am signing on. For a fee I will get all the advice I will want on any doggy subject. And so I am searching but soon realize that the personal interaction is missing and too many questions remain unanswered. I am finding another promising dog training program and I sign up for this one too. I need all the help I can get. Luckily this site had some great advice and puppy training videos I could use immediately on Harper. I am eager and determined to have Harper grow into a well behaved dog and to be the companion Bob and I were looking for. The common thread is patience, patience and some more patience is needed for a new puppy. It's only been a couple of weeks since we brought Harper home and my patience is still going strong. At our first vet visit Dr. Reed smiled and tells me to love him and be "patient".

As more time goes by and Harper not only exercises his teeth on my hands, feet, and shoes my patience is beginning to wear thin. Between 4:00 am to 6:00 am in the morning and immediately after dinner there is not a moment of peace in our house. We have an out of control puppy terrorizing us. If we are not bundling up to take him outside, cleaning the floor, then we are chasing after shoes and socks, fending off his still razor sharp baby teeth from biting my hands and toes. It is quite exhausting. We definitely don't sit on the couch watching TV anymore! As a matter of fact, we would love to sit down and watch a program but it seems pretty much impossible. Tension begins to rise and Harper is banned to the kitchen where he is rattling the gate trying to get out. There is no escape from this dog. Help! This is nerve wrecking. We are tired from getting up several times during the night and numerous trips outside in the cold winter days and nights. Deciding to go to bed early becomes the answer to a dog who will not allow for a minute of peace and quiet, only to start the cycle again a few hours later. This is a puppy on steroids. Will this ever end and how soon? My husband and I are tired and worn out by this little monster dog. We are both stressed and it shows. Bob can't wait to escape to work in the morning. Reading as much on the subject as I can is keeping me motivated and sane. One piece of advice I found about puppy biting is to give him ice cubes to crunch on. It is supposed to help the puppy with the chewing and much like a teething ring for a baby will feel good on his gums. I am willing to try anything and to my surprise Harper likes the ice cubes. Now at age eight months …. Harper comes running at the sound of the ice maker – my dog thinks it is a special treat and now seems to be addicted to ice cubes!!

I need help! Talking with as many dog owners as possible, I found out that most have kennel trained their dogs and don't have nearly the same complaints we do. Still, my husband is opposed. Why? I am sensing that he is starting to regret the decision to get a puppy and I am willing to try anything to make this work. Still searching the internet I found one site promising great results with clicker training. And so I purchase another dog training course. Everything I read and listen to makes great sense and I actually have some good luck with some of the training. At least Harper begins to pay attention and Baxter the cat can eat his food without being chased. However, it does not help with the chewing and the pure wildness of this dog. Our living room has become a race track for the dog. In addition Harper shows some aggression towards me when correcting him. He growls and shows his teeth and still uses them on my hands. He thinks he is boss. Oh boy, I am really not prepared for this and don't know what to do to tame this dog. Does he even like me? This constant biting and challenging me is getting old. I too was beginning to think it was a mistake getting a puppy. Why did I ever want a puppy? I had no idea it would be so challenging. However, giving up the dog was not an option. We need help – we need obedience training!

Comparing notes with my friend Debra she cannot remotely relate to my problems or I to hers. She has her own unique challenges with her new rescue dog which includes pottying in the house. While her dog is not a puppy she too has her work cut out for herself. Just like me – patience is the name of the game for her too. Neither of us can be any help to the other but it still feels good to encourage and talk it through. Apparently my desperation must have come through because she wants to know if I love the dog. Looking into my heart to find the true answer I find that "yes" I do love this little monster despite his untamed and wild manners.

Our son Chris comes to visit the puppy for the first time and I am in for a surprise. After sniffing and checking him out, Harper decides Chris is cool and declares him his new best friend. Together they sit on the floor and Harper is the best little puppy I could ask for. What is wrong with this dog? Why can't he do this with me? He is still biting at me at every touch and my hands and arms bear the marks. I am encouraged and have hope for the dog and us.

Another Challenge

Debra Wagner

My next big challenge with Cricket was separation anxiety.

Because I am always home, once Cricket had graduated from full-time sling duty, it was time to teach her how to be alone. You have to understand that these dogs had NEVER been alone in their lives- caged with hundreds of other dogs. The first time I left Cricket I went down to collect the mail. By the time I returned in about five minutes, Cricket was shivering and panting, and frothing at the mouth. Oh dear, this wouldn't work at all. I started noticing that when I would take a bath at night to soak my sore leg, Cricket would come in and lay on my lounge dress. She would stay there after fluffing it up to her satisfaction, and keep it warm for me until I exited the bath. Ah-ha! A method to the madness! When I was ready to leave the apartment I would change my clothes- and I took to putting my lounge dress in Cricket's bed so that she could lay on it while I was gone. Soon she understood what I was doing and began walking to the dress in her bed before I had even left. Success never tasted so good!!

So now I have begun to believe that I have finally trained my dog. I took Cricket in for her first grooming appointment- it felt strange leaving without her. Whenever I took her somewhere with me I still used the baby sling that she hated. When I went back to pick up the pretty baby, I left the sling in the car, thinking I could just put her in the front seat of the cart since I had to buy more dog food. She got in the cart seat and sat down with no problem while we paid for our food and then we went out the door to the parking lot. Suddenly a loud noise- and with no warning Cricket jumped right out of the cart and onto the parking lot! I don't know who was more surprised. She started to run towards an oncoming van and my heart was in my throat. I bolted after her and caught her in my arms just in time. We got in the car and I don't know whose heart was racing faster- hers or mine! I guess what the rescue guy said was true- you never know when they are going to bolt and run.

In the midst of all this doggy drama I heard from Birgit that she had finally found a dog to add to her family- I was so excited for her! She sent me a picture of the new little boy and told me that he was half Great Pyranees and half Labrador. To which I replied- did you MEAN to do that? She assured me that she did and that she and Bob were thrilled with their new addition to the family.

Which got me thinking- I sure did miss Kentucky. By now I had been in Colorado for two years, and the leg and my heart were telling me that this was not where I belonged. For heavens' sake, none of the restaurants here even served sweet tea! I really wanted to go home- but had no idea how I could possibly make it happen. And then- a Christmas miracle! The money fell out of the sky and into my lap. All of a sudden everything started falling into place. I went and talked to my apartment manager who graciously changed my 12 month lease into a 6 month lease. Birgit went and looked at the apartment complex she had told me about and said the apartments were gorgeous- brand new. I began communicating with the apartment manager and sent in my application for residency- and I was approved! I asked the manager, Amy, to send me my new address, and low and behold, I was going to live on Cricket Lane!! WOW- that was no coincidence!

So as dreams turned into plans and plans turned into reality, by the beginning of May I was back home in Kentucky. Birgit and I re-connected and returned to our mall-scoping, purse hunting, pizza-eating ways. I meandered (in the south we meander, we never hurry!) back to my friends Donna and Kelly on Park Avenue, where we sat on the front porch drinking our wine and catching up on the news of all the neighbors. And my little Cricket?

Help!
Birgit Stubblefield

One day on my way to work I decide to stop by Sam Russell's Pet Supply. I drive by there every day and know they offer an array of services. One of the services is doggy day care. I never really thought much about doggy day care but knew Debra took Lily once a week to this service. Lily always had a good time and liked going there very much. My first visit to Sam Russell's left me with a great impression. My first thought that this was "Cracker Barrel for Dogs". The store is rustic and inviting and the people are warm and I know my dog will be in good hands. At Sam Russell's, I meet Debbie and we have a long conversation about the challenges of puppy training. Debbie too preaches patience. Yes, I try to be patient but how much longer? Harper is not yet ready to come for a visit. First he will need all his puppy shots completed. Awwww....I am so ready for him to go and play with other dogs. We will need to wait another month or so. I leave assured that when he is ready to join daycare, he will be so tired when I bring him home that a very quiet evening is almost guaranteed. Oh, how I am longing for a couple of hours with a tolerable dog.

It has been a long time since my husband and I seriously fought over anything and ending up being mad at each other for more than one hour. Well, it happened - we had a fight over Harper. We were so stinking mad at each other for the entire day and night over a training collar I bought for Harper.

A dog collar of all things! Watching all these different training videos I decided that Harper needed a prong collar. At this time he was just about four months old and already developed a strange behavior.

He seemed to be afraid of the outside. No matter what we did, it got worse instead of better. Whenever we grabbed the leash to take him outside his ears would pin back and his tail would be between his legs. His favorite hiding place was under the dining room table or to simply run away. To say the least it was so frustrating to get a leash on him and it was nearly impossible to get him to come out of the house. We had to pick him up and carry him to the yard. No amount of treats would coax him out of the house.

Once in the yard he was mostly okay as long as nothing was out of the ordinary and no strange noises or unfamiliar shapes startled him. The first time he experienced a helicopter flying close by, he tucked tail and bolted.

Running straight to the door, he would sit in front of the door waiting for me to catch up. He would run for his life when a car drove by, the garbage truck or school bus passed or the neighbor dog barked.

Harper was filled with fear of anything strange and unknown. At the first sign of the unknown he runs and sits at the front door begging to go inside. Harper is four months and has never been on a walk or shows any interest in going for a walk. So much for my long walks I was hoping for. The short trip to the mailbox appears to be a horrifying experience. Passing the boat in the drive way is a huge obstacle and can only be achieved by taking a wide berth around it. Harper pulls so hard on the leash straining to get back to the house that I think I will need shoulder surgery.

At this point I am still carrying him out of the house but this is more difficult with his ever increasing weight. After all, he is going to be a big dog and has already more than doubled in size and weight. That's was when I decided to buy this prong collar to train him to walk with me. Although I read that these collars should not be used on puppies under six months, I was not going to use it in a harsh way but to give Harper a little more guidance and structure. Perhaps this would help! Bob was having none of this. He was dead set against the prong collar and our dog was not going to wear one. This collar reminded him of a medieval torture device; similar to the devices we saw in torture chambers of German castles we toured. He simply did not want to hear any of the great training advice I picked up online or that the collar supposed to resemble a quick nip much like the puppy's mother would use to teach her pups. After all, I did all the reading and planning and what did he do to ease the situation? Frustration was running high and tempers flared.

Stomping off downstairs to the man cave the standoff had begun. Neither was willing to talk about how to handle the dog – while I thought tough love was best Bob just threw up his hands and gave up. We were so mad, at each other and the dog. This was not good. Searching for the solution I resigned myself to giving up Harper and finding him a new home if this would help to restore normalcy back into our lives. I knew in my heart Bob was not happy and did not like his new life with this dog. As the day went on and evening settled in Bob found himself in the "doghouse". This is the first time in many years he elected to keep his distance and stay away from me and the dog. We went to bed mad at each other. After a long night and several trips out into a cold winter night along with cleaning the kitchen floor–handling everything by myself while Bob is snoozing in the basement–we finally came face to face by the coffee pot. Both feeling sorry about how things went the previous day, I tearfully offered to find a new good home for Harper but Bob would not want to hear any of it. The steam was out and we would make it work. I recognized that the dog already had a leash on my emotions and I already loved him and would be heartbroken to give him up – despite his unbelievable puppy manners. And with that the prong collar was not mentioned again. Looking back I know that we both were simply at our wits end. Fatigued and not knowing exactly what to do with this monster dog we let it get the better of us.

One morning walking by Sabo's grave I stopped and asked Sabo to stop playing in dog heaven for just a moment and take this puppy under his dog wings to guide and mentor him to be the dog we so desperately wanted. I felt silly confessing to Bob my early morning conversation with Sabo. Imagine my surprise when Bob confessed to having had the same conversation with Sabo.

Right around that time another surprise is coming my way – my friend Debra decided to move back to Kentucky! The long and hard winters in Colorado were just getting a little too much and what better place to go home to than where you hang your heart in the first place? My friend would return and color would come back into my life!!!

At four months old and only one immunization away from joining puppy care, I also made the decision to enroll Harper in obedience school at the earliest class available. First, I called Bella Gaudette, owner of Bella's K-9 Academy to set up a private class. I met Bella a couple of years earlier and met her incredibly well trained Border Collies. I wanted Harper to become the best trained dog so I too could take him to my office and stay with me without being a nuisance to my customers and coworkers. When arriving at the training facility for my private class I walked into an ongoing training session and was completely in awe about what I saw and the skills this dog displayed. I knew I had arrived at the right place. Bella has made quite a name for herself as trainer and my veterinarian also gave me her business card when I asked about a referral. Bella started working with her first dog in the early 80's, got her first Border Collie in 1992 and started training with the E'town Dog Training Club. Quickly she began teaching with the club until they disbanded. Dr. Brown with the Helmwood Veterinary Clinic asked Bella to continue her teaching at their facility until Dr. Brown encouraged her to start her own training facility in 2000. Bella has been training and showing her Border Collies since 1993 and has been training too many dogs to count. Affiliated with APDT, a Mentor Trainer for Animal Behavior College and CGC Educator she was just the right person to teach my dog some manners. It felt good to open up to Bella about the frustrations and helpless feeling we experienced. It was great having a professional dog trainer giving a mini class into the mind of a puppy and to set realistic expectations about the puppy stages. After all Harper was still a puppy. I learned about how to start Harper walking on a leash and some basic commands I could work on. Finishing class I was excited again and looked forward to teaching my dog some good behaviors.

The following week Harper went to puppy care for the first time. As usual, he was pulling and straining and not happy about being dragged to a strange place. The way he acted he must have thought about being dragged to a house of horrors. Leaving him there for an afternoon I knew it would be good for him but yet it felt a little bit like abandonment. When I picked Harper up a few hours later I was greeted by a very happy puppy which showed immediately by a big puddle on the floor. The great folk at Sam Russell's assured me that this happens all the time. Oh boy, this puppy was happy to go home – and immediately went to his dog bed and passed out. WOW! Debbie at Sam Russell told me this would happen! Bob and I had a GREAT evening - we actually watched an entire program for the first time in weeks. After just two visits Harper could not wait to get to puppy care. Before long we were hooked on puppy care, our insurance policy to a tired and happy puppy. Slowly but surely things started to calm down and we settled into a new routine.

Sibling Rivalry

Debra Wagner

Things are beginning to settle into a routine by now - finally we are all becoming adjusted to each other and this new situation. Dooney, though, remains unconvinced - it seems her new favorite pastime is sitting in the hallway and just hissing at the world in general. Okay, I get it- having a new baby in the house that seems to get all the attention can definitely create some tensions. I know that any new Mom out there can relate to trying to fulfill all the duties of a new little one in the home and still give attention to the older child. I believed that if I gave it some more time things would all just fall into place of their own accord. Wow, was I wrong!

One morning I was in the bathroom and I heard a loud commotion in the kitchen followed by Dooney tearing down the hallway and under the bed. What the hell had just happened? I walked into the kitchen and saw Cricket picking through her food just like normal. There were some kibble on the floor - was this the sign of a scuffle? Time to get out my detective gear and find out!

That night after I had filled both their bowls with kibble, I watched from a corner of the room as Cricket went in to eat. As I waited a moment or two, Dooney came out of the bedroom and began sauntering her way to the kitchen. Just a few steps at a time, gingerly, slowly moving forward to the bowl of dog kibble. So it seems that Dooney has gone from waiting patiently for leftovers to coveting the kibble right away. Could this be the reason for all that noise this morning?

As Dooney finally reached the bowl that Cricket was eating out of, Dooney moved her head in front of Cricket as she was bending down to get more food. Then - it happened! Quick as a snake Cricket lunged at Dooney and growled at her - the message was clear - get away from my food!! Oh, no - food aggression; this was not good. I was aware that in her previous life Cricket probably did not have enough to eat and more than likely had to fight to keep her food. But that was the old life - and this is the new one where the kibble dish is always full. So I calmly walked into the kitchen, and touched Cricket's neck with two fingers and sternly said "No!" Her reaction was instantaneous - she emitted a pitiful cry and rolled over and exposed her belly in the submissive position. Oh dear, I felt like the worst doggy Mom in the world - you would think I had beaten her! Okay, maybe a little softer in the tone, but still a correction that was obviously needed. So for the next few days I had to stand guard over the mealtimes. I felt like one of those English bobbies who guard the castle and cannot say a word or move - holding still so I could see what was going to happen. As time wore on Dooney finally decided to wait until Cricket was done with her food again, so the aggression issue was over.

Or was it?? Another difficulty that had arisen was Mom's lap time for the kids. Obviously both Cricket and Dooney were used to sitting in my lap while I was watching TV, but never at the same time. In the beginning after bringing Cricket home, Dooney was too annoyed to consider sitting in my lap with that THING. As time wore on she realized that the new fuzzy creature was not going to leave Mom's lap anytime soon and she was just going to have to deal with it. So she made her play. Very slowly Dooney made her way halfway onto my lap - and then it happened again! The lunge, the growl - instant repeat and a new form of aggression - Mom aggression. This was not acceptable either. Two fingers to the neck, another (less stern) "No!" and Dooney bounded down from the chair. Cricket did not like the idea of sharing her new Mom with anyone and it showed. Which means I had to work on that patience thing that the vet had told me about, and continue to correct Cricket when she lunged at Dooney. And unfortunately this went on for many nights to come.

Poor Dooney - I give her lots of credit for continuing to try and make it onto my lap. One of the things that I learned was to remain very still and let the interaction play out without any interference from Mom unless needed. What was that they taught me in drama class? Oh right - BE the chair, BECOME the chair. No emotions, no reactions, just be the big overstuffed red chair that has become the arena for these two tiny gladiators. Be very still and silently observe. Night after night Dooney kept trying, Cricket kept lunging, and I kept correcting. Until finally one night Dooney waited until Cricket was asleep - Dooney came in and turned around and settled onto my lap being careful not to touch Cricket. BE the chair. No emotions - no movement! There - she did it!! For a whole hour we all sat together in the chair without confrontation. And Dooney was the one who decided to get down, not being forced out like usual. This was wonderful!!

It was a few nights later that again Cricket was in my lap and Dooney sought refuge there as well. (I am BEING the chair again.) Dooney gracefully leapt up into my lap and lay down. Cricket kind of snuffled but then turned her head away. As a few more moments passed I could hear the soft sounds of Cricket's breathing and knew she was asleep. As I looked down I couldn't believe it- Oh, is it really possible? - Dooney was licking Cricket's back - she was GROOMING Cricket!! And more importantly, Cricket was letting her! As a smile broke across my face, I thought to myself - "Has a chair ever been so happy?"

It's All Good

Birgit Stubblefield

Potty training started to come along. Harper eventually discovered piddle pads and later jumped on the door when he needed to go. Our nights got more restful. We actually got a few hours of sleep before getting up to let Harper go outside. Seemingly all of a sudden Harper slept through an entire night without an accident or waking us up. The pride and joy can only be compared to potty training a child who finally "got" it.

It is March now and obedience training is set to begin. Not sure what to expect Bob and I meet at Bella's K-9 Academy along with several other frazzled dog owners. The class consists of a couple of German Shepherds, a rowdy little Boxer puppy, a mild mannered Shih Tzu and an adorable Golden Retriever girl named Molly Rose. We have our work cut out for us. Every week we have homework assignment and for eight weeks I love to go to see the progress all the dogs are making. Bella is a great teacher – tough but loving and compassionate. Her knowledge of training methods and dog psychology is priceless. I try to soak it all up but it seems so much to do and to remember. At class it quickly becomes apparent that truly the dog owners are the ones being trained rather than the dogs. We are being trained how to handle our dogs and teach them basic commands. Harper seems to enjoy coming to class as much as I do – Bob not so much.

One day early in the week I received a phone call from Dr. Reed that a neutering appointment just came open for the next day. With no hesitation, I agreed to bring Harper in the next day to get snipped provided he could continue with his training. When I picked him up, Harper did not slow down. Although we were supposed to keep him from running and jumping, Harper just acted as if nothing happened and he was ready for his mischief. He did not miss any class and did not show any signs of slowing down. Little by little and almost without being noticed, Harper begins to change.

Eight weeks later, we wrap up class and Harper, along with the other dogs, passes a final "test" of all commands he has learned. All dogs passed the class and Bella had a little graduation cere-mony. Each dog received his certificate, a dog treat and a picture. I thought it was great and I felt like a proud Mama. The pictures were taken during training by a very talented pet photographer – Debbie - who is also a student of Bella's K-9 academy at a different level and class. At the very least I would recommend a basic obedience class to anyone with a new dog. We enjoyed obedience training so much that I immediately enrolled us into the Level II course just a few weeks later.

In the meantime we practice at home as much as we can and time allows. Bob leaves very early in the morning for work and I am so busy at my job that I always seem to chase time but never really catch it. Puppy care is the best invention for working puppy parents which we take full advantage of. We love Sam Russell's! Still around 8:00 pm every night – we can almost set a clock to it – Harper turns into a wild thing. Usually this does not last too long so we have learned to deal with it. By now he is housebroken and goes outside without being bribed. Actually, he is beginning to explore the outside more and is slowly becoming accustomed to different noises, although he still does not like to go any further than the mailbox. We walk him on a leash in the backyard for training and to keep him from getting into trouble.

By now the weather has changed from icy cold to wet and slushy. After one rainy night I am walking with Harper very early morning in our back yard; it is sill dark and I am still half asleep. He is on a 20 feet retractable leash so he can wander around. He is so mild mannered this morning and walks so beautifully beside me that my mind begins to wander. I am not paying too much attention to what he is doing or sniffing at. Somewhere far down the road a truck engine starts up and in that same instance my dog turns into a race horse. He takes off running – all I remember seeing is a white streak. I am holding on to the leash for dear life. Harper, even though still a puppy, has developed an incredible strength and by now is pulling me hard. Not wanting to let go of the leash I stumble in the dark, running into tree branches, trip over tree roots to be stopped in my tracks by a good size holly. While falling to the ground I know I twisted my ankle badly. Did I mention the leash instructions came with a warning and website instruction how to avoid the exact thing I regrettably experienced? Well, yes…I read the warning signs and I watched the video too! At this point I let go of the leash to avoid being dragged on the ground. I am pulling myself off the ground and immediately know this is not good. Hobbling to the door my dog is sitting pretty as he pleases by the door waiting to get inside. I am hurt terribly and am close to tears but this one is on me – not the dog. In no way did I scold Harper or was mad; he simply did what his instinct told him to do. He felt in danger and he took off for safety. The trust between human and animal was still fragile and not yet solid. It would take much longer before Harper would trust his human leader. My lesson for the day was that we were still a long way from our goal and I needed to pay attention to my dog and what he was doing. The following three days I could not even step on my foot - swollen big and turning black and blue it would take a total of seven weeks before my foot was back to normal. Taking Harper out was impossible for me so the entire burden was on Bob. Once again we relied heavily on Sam Russell for puppy care.

In the meantime Debra has moved back home to Elizabethtown and we are living just a stone's throw away from each other. As if no time has passed when we see each other for the first time in a couple of years, we pick up where we left without missing a beat. Debra is her colorful self and our friendship is intact and thriving. Our dogs have not met yet – as Debra likes to point out, Harper's head is as big as her entire dog. Cricket may be an afternoon snack for Harper. Cricket is a sweet little soul and she is one of the lucky dogs. Lucky that she was adopted by Debra.

By now it is June; Harper has been with us for a full six months. He has slowed down and he is beginning to settle down. Our nights are peaceful and we can sleep again without any nightly potty calls from the dog. My kitchen floor doesn't smell like salad dressing anymore. It is much warmer and we enjoy taking Harper outside for a game of Tennis ball or Frisbee. He loves to chase and to be chased. It is a joy to have this dog around us. He has gotten big – 63 pounds and counting. I love the way he sits so proudly under his favorite tree. Every day he reminds us more and more of Sabo. The way he sits, pays attention to us, loves to see us when we pick him up. Harper has turned into a sweet boy who resembles another dog we so dearly loved. Of course I contribute his behavior change to growing up and maturing, neutering and obedience training but perhaps a little voice guided him from dog heaven…?

Growing Up

Birgit Stubblefield

Level II obedience classes are ready to start. I am ready and look forward to what comes next. I am excited but again don't know for sure what we'll be doing. All I know is that we are going to prove what we have learned in Level I. After the first class I am hooked. I know Harper will enjoy it too. This turns out to be so much more fun and hands on training than Level I. Perhaps it only appears this way but all the questions I had before seem to be answered in this course. My dog knows how to sit and how to stay but the big question is how one enforces this in any environment and over longer periods of time. How do I get my dog to walk beside me (heel) and how do I get him to listen to me when I am asking him to follow a command? This is the good stuff – at least for me. After all, I vowed to have the best behaved dog in Elizabethtown, next to Bella's of course. And so the fun begins and will continue for eight weeks. At the beginning of class Bella announces that a weekly challenge will be issued and a test will be given during the following class. Each performance will be rated and every dog meeting the challenge within two tries will receive a star. The dog with the most stars at the end of class will receive a prize. Now I think this is such a clever way to ensure the dog owners will work with their dogs throughout the week. I think this is a fabulous idea and I already love it. What people usually don't think when they first meet me is that I am fiercely competitive. Outwardly quiet and polite, I have a fire burning inside my belly.

All my life people have told me I can't do this or that - starting with moving from one continent to another many years ago. I was told I don't speak the language and I that will be homesick. Well, I proved everyone wrong. I am speaking the English language fluidly although with an accent still – I am continuously working on that. I was told I would not find a job – well I went back to school to increase my hiring ability and started with a minimum wage job. From there I worked my way up to branch manager of a finance company. When I decided to enter the mortgage world I was told I was not the right material for this competitive field and would be back within six months begging for my old job. It has been ten years and I am the top producer throughout several of these years. So, to give my dog a challenge to win a prize I am taking this to the next level and the challenge is on. I am so excited because not only do I want to meet the challenge but I sincerely want to teach my dog – after all this is why we signed up. Our first assignment is to instruct our dogs to lay down on command.

Per Bella this is a hard assignment since the down position is a very submissive position and the dog may not easily want to follow the command. So, no sooner do we get home, we are starting on training. It is a nice Saturday afternoon and we incorporate plenty of play time and treats to make the hard learning just a little bit easier – on both of us. It is not long at all that Harper understands what I am asking him to do. He also knows from experience that he is going to be highly praised and rewarded. I think it makes him feel good to please me – but perhaps he only wants the treats. We work throughout the day and every day during the week. We practice first thing in the morning and last thing at night. Harper's got this, no doubt.

Saturday comes by fast and we are all lined up in class again. This class is small, only five of us. This makes the course fun as the dog owners come together and form a loose bond. The moment of truth – the challenge is up. Who wants to go first? No one wants to, so what the heck Harper and I volunteer.

We step out and I give him the command "Harper down" and Harper lays down as beautiful as a picture, on the first try!!! My heart swells, I am so proud of my dog I want to jump out of my skin. When the competition is over Harper is the only dog getting his star on his first try.

I am so excited when I get home and tell Bob all about it that it is hard to contain myself. I still feel like I want to burst with pride of my mutt's accomplishments. I want to tell the world about it and so the idea of sharing this short story with potential new dog owners is starting to form. Sharing the tribulations and triumph to encourage everyone thinking about adopting a dog – weather buying from a breeder or adopting from a shelter – that love and patience really are the answers. Harper is the only mixed breed in class and he will never be a show dog. But he will be the smartest, well trained, well behaved and most loved dog in my world. We still have a long way to go and this is only challenge number one but he is already a winner in my book.

Harper's Career?

Birgit Stubblefield

At the final class of Level II we have the option to get our dogs Canine Good Citizen (CGC) certified. Harper can participate but is not old enough to be awarded his certificate. CGC certified dogs are just one step under a certified therapy dog. Just for fun and to find out if we would pass the test we are going to participate. Perhaps when Harper has reached his first birthday I will sign him up to train for this therapy dog certification.

Sad recent circumstances led me to think about Harper being trained as a therapy dog early on. About three weeks after we brought Harper home we took our first long distance car trip to visit Bob's family in his Tennessee hometown. His Dad had been admitted to a nursing home several months earlier due to a debilitating illness that would only get worse over time. Ridden with Alzheimer's and Parkinson's disease, Dad's world had shrunk to his wheelchair and his room and his interest in everyday things began to wane along with his desire to communicate. During our Christmas visit we shared the news with him that we were getting a new dog and thanks to smart phones we were able to show him a picture of Harper. It was so heartwarming to see how Dad's face lit up and a big smile formed when he saw the picture on the screen. He seemed happy and he wanted to meet Harper. We were determined to make his wish come true. The nursing home was great and allowed us to bring Harper provided his shots were up to date and we could bring a picture of Harper to be displayed in Dad's room. The picture was meant to let staff know this dog was allowed to visit.

Our trip to Tennessee was uneventful. The dog did great – actually I chose to sit on the back seat and hold him in my lap. This was the only time he would allow me to hold him without biting me all the time. I so much enjoyed this trip and almost wished it would not end so soon. Harper was great and visiting with Mom went great. Clearly he enjoyed all the attention he was getting and of course Mom was prepared to bribe the dog with a big batch of "yum yum's; the treats Mom had waiting for him.

Off to the nursing home we went to see Dad and introduce his new grand dog. Walking down the long hallway, Harper and Bob both respectively pulling on the leash, we passed a number of residents. Without exceptions everyone, including staff, was delighted to see this little puppy and stopped to pet this cute little thing. When entering Dad's room it was as if we did not even exist. Dad had eyes only for the puppy and the smile on his face told us he was happy to have this furry visitor. Gently we placed Harper on his lap holding him as still as we could until it was time to go home. From this visit forward we made sure to bring Harper to the nursing home every time we visited. Without fail every time it made Dad's day to pet Harper; and without fail everyone in the nursing home wanted to pet him too. As Dad's illness progressed and he no longer spoke he would still light up at the sight of Harper and would touch his picture on the smart phone screen. Now I have heard of therapy dogs but did not know much about what is required of them, or what impact their visit to a nursing home or hospital would have on the residents. On that first visit to meet Dad the seed was planted to perhaps look into a career for Harper to become a therapy dog. It is heartwarming to know that while the lights dimmed in Dad's brain our furry little kid brought some of the light back, if only for a short time. I will say that Dad was buried with Harpers picture and may he have found peace in heaven – perhaps with another one of his grand dogs by his side.

Home Sweet Home
Debra Wagner

By now Cricket has settled into being a member of our family. After six months, with many tiny bits of hot dog as incentive, she has finally learned how to "sit". I know that may not sound like much, especially with Harper at the head of the obedience class, but "sit" for Cricket has required a lot of patience, and more patience, and hot dogs. (With Dooney circling like a great white shark looking for any leftover tidbits) Cricket proudly walks on her leash outside and plows through the grass as tall as she is to potty. (Think of a marine in camouflage creeping through the underbrush and you get the idea!) Cricket can still poop faster than a speeding bullet, and when Dooney does her business it is always a race between me and Cricket to see who can get there first. Cricket still thinks that "Come" is more of a suggestion than a command, but we are working on it. She loves people, which I was concerned about in light of her abuse. She is indeed a sweetheart-

anyone who comes over is subject to that little nibbly tail wagging and that cute face begging to be picked up. Cricket and Dooney have come to an understanding, although being a human I am still not quite certain what the terms are. I am so thankful that I hung in there on the days when I cleaned up yet ANOTHER piddle spot for the 17th time that day, and had to chase her down with a kitty turd in her mouth spilling kitty litter all the way. Even though I could not imagine having another dog after Lily, I have come to realize that we are blessed to have many opportunities in our lives for love. I can still remember the day I gave myself permission to fall in love with Cricket. She had fallen asleep in my lap, and began to very quietly snore- barely discernible to my ears. I looked down at that tiny being in my lap, and looked up into doggy heaven, and thanked Lily for sending me a dog that had a quieter snore.

Lucky
Birgit Stubblefield

Photo courtesy of D. Smith Photos@2013

Today was graduation day from Level II obedience training for Harper and our final challenge was to be evaluated. Vacation has gotten in the way to complete class per schedule but Bella was gracious and allowed us to come early to complete the Canine

Good Citizenship test requirements. Testing contains a set of ten different tasks which Harper performed beautifully and once again made me a proud Mom. One of the tasks was to meet and greet another person who also happens to be out on a walk with her dog. During this short meet and greet the student dog is supposed to show good behavior by not pulling on his leash, trying to engage the other dog or showing too much interest in the other dog while the owners stop, shake hands and have a short conversation. My partner for this exercise – a person I never met before – shook my hand and her words to me were "You have a very beautiful dog, you are lucky he found you". Indeed I am very lucky that Harper chose me to become his Mom.

On to our final challenge – we completed and passed the difficult task for a short off leash heeling but did not quite as well as during our practice time at home. At time of writing I believe we are still in the competition to win a price but the race is tight. Furthermore should there be a tie we won't be there for the tiebreaker challenge. No matter, my dog is already a winner! However, it was a lot of fun to be part of this class and having fun while teaching our dogs good manners is what it is all about. Have fun with it! To find out about the final competition results and other great information visit Bella's K-9 Academy on Facebook or send e-mail to:

HarperandCricket@gmail.com.

Please consider your local shelter or animal rescue for the pick of your next life companion. All dogs are creatures who love to love and please their owners when given the proper environment and of course love.

Resources:

Petfinder.com

Breederadoptions.org

Pet Connection NKY: www.ky.petfinder.com

Hardin County Animal Control: 270- 360-9460

Helmwood Veterinary Clinic:
  www.helmwoodvet.com

Heartland Veterinary Hospital:
  www.animalhospital@heartlandveterinary.com

Bella's K-9 Academy: www.bellask9.com

Sam Russell's Pet Provisions:
  www.samrussellspetprovisions.com

Buried Treasure: Hardin County Pet Protection 270-360-9460 - Offers spay-neuter assistance to approved low income families

P.A.W.S.: http://pawsdonations.org

D.Smith Photos – Pet Photography
  www.dsmithphotos.vpweb.com

CPSIA information can be obtained at www.ICGtesting.com
Printed in the USA
LVOW01s0816171113

361624LV00003B/149/P

9 781937 508210